OUT OF KILTER

SOCIETAL PROGRAMS GONE AWRY

They Promised Us the Moon
Volume III

BY

WILLIAM PARKER ARCHIBALD

OUT OF KILTER
They Promised Us the Moon– Volume III

Copyright © 2015 by William Parker Archibald

Textual Advisement: Elaine Bush
Technical Support: Digital Depot (Maurice Tift)
Editing: Kit Duncan
Book Layout: Nat Mara

A writer should struggle with the words
so the reader won't have to.

– the author

When I was a youngster,

My father's favorite joke was about the farmer who had a pig with a wooden leg. When asked about it, the farmer went on for days about the virtues of the pig and how attached the family had become to it.

Acknowledging all of that, the visitor asked yet again why the animal had a wooden leg. To which the farmer responded, "Well, if you had a pig like that, would you eat it all at once?"

This, in a real way, is the story of America. I'm not questioning our love for it. That is well established. Rather, I'm questioning why, after centuries of toil and sacrifice, we've all of a sudden turned on it and are now devouring it with the reckless abandon of fools who sat down to feast on the goose that laid the golden egg.

Dedication

This book, indeed this whole endeavor to preserve, protect and defend that which has been given to us at such enormous cost, is dedicated to all of the patriots, both living and dead and to my good friend and mentor,

Millard Fuller,
founder of Habitat for Humanity International and the Fuller Center for Housing.

OUT

OF

KILTER

The War on Poverty

Won't Be Over Until

People Are Autonomous,

Self Directed

And Most Importantly

Self Sufficient.

Continuing Forward!

Thanks to the bravery and life work of the Reverend Dr. Martin Luther King Junior, blacks are finally in the house. That's great! Wonderful! Yet, the work is far from over.

It won't so much as begin to near completion until we stop enabling, allow for the assumption of responsibility and begin to transition people from the kiddie table into the real, adult world of self-reliance.

They obviously can do it. We just have to step aside a bit and let them cut their own meat and make their own decisions while we actively cheer them on.

It'll require a collective effort, but that's O.K. We're all in this together. After all, we truly are part of "the Human Family."

Dangerously Out Of Kilter

The first, very first, thing God did was work an honest week. It's true! Dedication to the task became pride of accomplishment, which was then followed by Sabbath rest. Wanting to share the joy, God immediately sent man to tend a garden that we, too, might reap the same benefits. Most of us get it. Most of us understand that the best feeling in the world is receiving good pay for a job done well.

Regrettably, however, there are those who don't. They skip over the part about working and want to go directly to rest. They want to enjoy the fruits of labor, just long as it's not their labor. So, they pile on and take a free ride on those who pull their weight through the sweat of their brow. Accordingly, honest wage earners are hit from all sides, both coming and going. On their shoulders, they carry the weight of employers and financiers whose bloated pay packages are often determined by their ability to deny fair compensation to those who have rightfully earned a decent living.

Then, coming from the exact opposite direction, but armed with the same combination of greed mixed with slothfulness, are those not at the top, but rather the absolute bottom, who contribute as little as possible, save their own bad life decisions, and then play on our sympathies, hoping and trusting we will have pity and perpetually support them. These individuals, directed by impulses and not long range planning, drop out of school, sabotage their lives, and have us care for them.

So, there we have it, those who rise early and faithfully go to work every day continue to lose ground because they are saddled with the weight of those perched on their shoulders and the weight of those clinging to their ankles as they trudge forward, just trying to make ends meet. Truly, folks caught in the middle are getting the rawest of deals.

We Need To Pause, Stand Back and Look at the Kind of Life We Have Created

Something is not right when people refrain from earning above a certain amount of money lest they lose their benefits. Yet, that is exactly what is happening today. Literally millions of Americans have counted the cost and determined it is in their best interest to remain just idle enough and poor enough for the rest of us to carry them in perpetuity.

Something is not right when companies refrain from hiring above a certain number of people lest they enter a new bracket that requires workers' comp and health insurance for their employees. Yet, there isn't a fledgling enterprise in this country that hasn't seriously considered holding itself back lest the cost of doing business becomes prohibitive.

Something is not right when people have to work at multiple jobs because their employers won't schedule them for more than 32 hours a week as a way of avoiding paying health coverage. Yet, it is happening more and more often in this land of opportunity.

Something is not right when American companies have to pay a major portion of their employees' insurance while competing against global rivals that don't, yet that is the reality in this "new world order" that Administration after Administration have pushed on us.

Something is not right when people do all of the right things, make all of the right choices, endure all of the right sacrifices, and work hard art-in and year-out only to end up homeless one day due to the loss of their jobs, and the subsequent loss of their medical benefits ... while others who have never worked a day in their lives or taken any responsibility for their actions, are guaranteed perpetual food, shelter, and limitless health care for themselves and their dependents. Yet, we see it all of the time.

I believe it is in everyone's best interest to have a country where we all work and play, live and die on the same level playing field, where the decisions we make have real consequences and create real opportunities.

Ultimately It All Boils Down to a Fork in the Road

Option I:

We can continue to develop larger and larger societal systems where all of our time, effort, and resources go into erecting and maintaining a massive network that supplies all of our needs or…

Option II:

We all try to simplify things at every level and make life as fair as possible so that each is person is afforded the opportunity to make the best out of his or her own personal life. The first approach of devising ever larger societal programs to fix our personal needs disempowers the individual as their power is funneled up to the top of the pyramid from which all decisions are made. The bigger the structure, the less personal decision making and freedom are tolerated.

I am of the opinion that the second option-- personal freedom—is better as it enhances drive and creativity instead of stifling them. It assumes the best of people instead of the worst and doesn't waste a majority of its efforts on crowd control and the policing of its own people.

To Regulate–Or Not To Regulate?

The Answer is Simple:

- *Regulate the things that are so big that people are powerless against them.*

- *Deregulate the things where doing so makes people more independent and self-reliant.*

For example:

We do need strictly enforced regulation of the business community, as without it, consumers are at their mercy. At the same time, we're best served by the deregulation of price and fare structures as this promotes competition and keeps the lid on price hikes.

Republicans: Listen Up!

No one can make sure that banks and Wall Street play by the rules; no one, save regulatory bodies that were created to do just that. When they fall asleep on the job, greed runs amuck and shady practices cause millions of people to lose their life savings.

We saw it happen in the Depression, the Savings and Loan debacle of the 1980s, the stock market crash that occurred later in the same decade and the mega real estate and stock market meltdown of 2006-8. Perhaps we will now take seriously the need to police those who handle our money.

Democrats: Listen Up!

Conversely, while we obviously do need large scale monitoring of large scale enterprises--lest the little guy gets trampled--the exact opposite is true when we as a society are tempted to get overly involved in the daily needs of people's personal lives.

The more society as a whole tries to step up and fix people, the more we see a large percentage of them draw back and allow us to do just that. In fact, it is becoming increasingly evident that when we "give a man a fish," we often not only end up feeding him for a day but an entire lifetime.

The reason for this is simple:

People know that the more we provide for them, the less they have to do to care for themselves. As a result, their economic situation often doesn't improve, but rather gets bogged down in ever deepening dependency. They come to wrongly misinterpret these unexpected blessings as an opening for working less.

Forgive the analogy, but this dynamic closely resembles the experience of park rangers at Yellowstone National Park. Over the years, bears were beginning to lose their natural ability to hunt because they were hanging around the campgrounds, eating freebies from the dumpsters. The more this went on, the more park rangers had to make drastic changes in their waste management practices--not for their sake or the tourists' sake, but for the sake of the bears.

The same principle applies here. We should have people take responsibility for their own lives and pay for the things they can personally afford. This will deter people from making irresponsible decisions and becoming dependent on the state for assistance.

What about Our Responsibility to the Poor?

I believe I do have some life experience here. I was raised in a middle class family in suburban Maryland. My father was a pastor and my mother was an elementary school music teacher. When I was 18, I moved to Koinonia Farm, a Christian Community seven miles outside of Americus, Georgia. (The name Koinonia comes from the Greek word for fellowship.)

While there, I got involved in a literacy program for youngsters and within a few months of my arrival, I moved into the poorest section of town and became a neighborhood big brother to the very kids I had been tutoring. I wanted to live on or below the economic level they did, so I supported myself by working part time at Hardee's.

I rented a concrete block shack for $20 a month that I affectionately called the Shady Rest. In looking back, I should have come up with a better name as there was little rest with the occasional freight trains running less than twenty feet from my front door. My furnishings consisted of one chair, a bureau, and a box spring on a bare concrete floor. I had no radio or television, just a single naked light bulb hanging from the ceiling, a sink that only ran cold water, and a flush toilet in the equivalent of an outhouse. I existed on one meal a day at the local college where, a couple of times a week, I sneaked the world's fastest showers. I don't know of a time when I've ever been happier.

Twice a week, "my kids" came over for Bible stories, refreshments and a hike to the library where the most wonderful staff in the world reached out and simply loved them. They read children's stories to them, put on puppet shows, and went out of their way to make sure every child got a library card whether the books were returned or not. In time, the Shady Rest became a bookmobile stop.

When Linda and Millard Fuller returned from a couple of years of building houses in Zaire, on behalf of the fellowship at Koinonia Farm, Millard opened a law practice and started a new global housing ministry. In exchange for painting his house, he offered to let me stay rent free in a back room of the office, thus making me (without ever working there) the very first resident of Habitat for Humanity.

Since then, my life has been largely about serving others. I have spent years working to provide adequate nutrition to impoverished seniors, words of hope to the incarcerated, and a way out for heroin addicts in the South Bronx, which at that time was described by ABC News as "the worst neighborhood in America." I have also been a pastor, promoter of organ and tissue donation, and a full time caregiver. Currently, I am back in Americus, Georgia, ministering to dying patients and their families as a full time hospice chaplain.

My home, the Shady Rest in Americus, Georgia, 1974

My Love Letter to
the Black Community

(Because It Was Written With Love)

One of the weirdest courses I ever took was taught by a former nun at a Unitarian seminary in Berkeley. It was one of the nine schools comprising Graduate Theological Union of which my school, Pacific School of Religion, was a member.

At the time, I remember thinking this woman had been smoking way too much weed, for while other professors came to class with lengthy lecture notes and lists of books for us to read, she had us put aside our notebooks and pens and do watercolors while she spoke to us about life. "Behold the options," she'd say, holding up two pieces of paper, one a clean, fresh sheet with nothing on it and another with word after word crossed out and written over. "Which is scarier for the writer?" she asked. "It's the clean sheet isn't it?" "Get in there and make a mess," she intoned, "for until you give yourself permission to screw things up, you'll never have the courage to attempt anything of significance."

As I look back, her class probably taught me more than many of the others combined for she encouraged her students to look at life from different perspectives. "Remember the chakras," she'd say, "Don't assume everyone is operating on the same chakra." Chakras, according to Eastern thought, are energy centers or zones located throughout the body. The higher the chakra, the more the emphasis is on things of the mind, the intellect, while the lower chakras stimulate the carnal, sensuous aspects of our being. Ideally, we should access all of these energy fields and not fixate on one region to the exclusion of others. Having said that, the reason, according to this system of thought, blacks are such great athletes and able to produce such soulful passion is their unique ability to access the deeper energy zones or chakras. Indeed, where would Gospel music, Jazz and Motown be without the contribution of blacks? They'd be stifled and dry, like New Orleans dialed back to the rhythmic equivalent of a Tulsa, Oklahoma.

You, my friends, are the seasoning that adds flavor to the stew and rescues us from the blandness of dull intellectual pursuits, the seductress that ignites the animal in us thereby making the domain of pleasure all the more pleasurable lest lives be lived only from the neck up. You are authentic, rooted in your humanity, the melodic voice that moves the entire body, the soulful emotion that weeps and wails loudly at funerals while others sit in stunned silence.

This is your contribution, your essence, a reminder to the rest of us that things of the heart are deep, beyond mere words the tongue can utter. The inherent risk of getting to these levels is, of course, that of getting stuck there or, even worse, being like the submarine that, unable to pull up from its descent, continues to dive until it reaches "crush depth," where it implodes into a thousand pieces.

Fifty years after Martin Luther King's March on Washington, I am profoundly saddened to hear so many in the black community now take pride in referring to themselves as "niggers, gangsters and thugs." This is not, mind you, like the practice of police departments that have taken the hate filled term "pigs" and reversed its meaning by saying it stands for P.I.G.S. or Police in Good Service. To the contrary, this is just the opposite. It is an affirmation of the very worst aspects of the designation.

I am particularly miffed at the entertainment industry. When I was a youngster looking at a map of the continental United States, I took it to resemble the picture of a dinosaur. Perhaps this is because, at the time, Sinclair Oil Company used a rough rendition of a dinosaur in their company emblem. Think about it. The head and eyes of the dinosaur are Washington, D.C. The front legs are the state of Florida, the hind legs that provide the power are Texas, the heart or bread basket is the mighty Midwest and just below where a tail would be attached is, what else, but Hollywood...thus explaining the excrement that it has put out in recent years. Tell me I am out of line here! I don't think so. They have taken impressionable youths and foisted upon them degenerate role models. This is particularly the case in the music industry where rap artists glorify guns and the gangster lifestyle, both of which are dead end streets.

Just within my brief lifetime, they have gone from producing such insightful, uplifting works of Sidney Poitier in "The Lilies of the Field" and "In the Heat of the Night" to sinking to giving an Academy Award for best music in 2006 to "It's Hard Out Here for a Pimp." That's quite a decline from "Raindrops Keep Falling on My Head", the winner in the same category in 1969.

I am old enough to remember that the best argument for segregation was that it was the only way the white community had to insulate itself from the guns, the drugs, and violence that at the time seemed endemic to the black community. Fortunately, this argument was trumped by the best argument for integration, namely that segregation closed the door to the countless number of good and decent people who were wrongly associated with such behaviors and had the right to themselves flee and live in better surroundings.

My fear is that with so many claiming the term "niggers" and identifying themselves as thugs and gangsters, this will only serve to justify a return to a negative racial profiling of the black community as a whole. I am sure that many in the white community could draw a comparison to the taking of Troy and the story of the Trojan Horse. The attackers were unable to breach the city's walls, so they constructed a massive wooden horse on wheels, left it outside the gates and drew back. Seeing that the assailants had left, those inside the fortress opened the gates and pulled in the wooden statue, then closed the gates again. In the middle of the night, while the city slept, soldiers hidden inside the horse opened the trap door, let themselves down to the ground, then ran and opened the gates and signaled for the attackers to return. Before the city's residents fully realized what was happening, their assailants had flooded in through the gates and brought down the city.

My fear is that taking pride at being "in the hood" will only spark revulsion on the part of those in the white community who still have their hoods neatly tucked away in bureau drawers waiting for a justification to go back to their previous practice of racial profiling. I mean, what argument can be put forth to those who say, "You see, you see! For fifty years we have taken down all of the barriers and drawn them in; and now that they are fully integrated, they show themselves for what we have always said they were, just a bunch of 'niggers.'"

Don't believe the lies of music moguls who seek to reap rich rewards at the expense of you reaching your full human potential. You are far more gifted, talented and able than sinking to the lowest forms of human behavior they wish to pin on you. Think about it, the word "rap" is used in only three places, all of them negative. First, there is taking the "rap" or blame, then there is a "rap sheet" that is slang for a criminal record and lastly, there is "rap music" which is a misguided glorification of antisocial behaviors that will eventually lead to your imprisonment and/or destruction. Rise up and seize the opportunities that are there for you, for me, for each of us. God has provided the ladder. It is now up to each of us to climb it. Own your soulful passions, but do not let them own you. Reach for the stars. We need you. We need each other.

And remember, if you seek to fit into any mold, be conformed in mind and spirit not to those who seek their own selfish goals at your expense, indeed your very freedom. Instead, run with absolute abandon to the other end of the spectrum, to the headwaters of limitless grace and ultimate success, to a love that does not drain or diminish, but rather from a posture of absolute sufficiency seeks only for you to know, to experience, to adopt for yourselves the truest of joys that can only be found in blessing each person and each situation you encounter. This is my deepest and highest prayer, not only for you, but also for me and for all of us. Be well.

The Death Knell of
the Human Spirit

From many years of trying to help others, I am more convinced than ever that there is only one surefire way to destroy people. Just assure them that regardless of whatever they do or don't do, they'll never go without. Then sit back and watch lives that should have thrived on ambition and determination disintegrate into idle self-destruction. It's been the ruin of many born into opulent wealth from time immemorial and now, in an equally misguided understanding of love and charity, we ladle out copious amounts of the same poison to children born into poverty.

Consequences in life are difficult to handle, yet without them we have no measurement, no scorecard to tell us if we're on track or off course. Softening life's realities by cushioning its blows might work in the short term, but what's going to happen when we aren't there to superimpose our concept of what reality should be on top of what reality already is?

Show Me a Life
Without Consequences,
and I'll Show You
An Inconsequential Life

Why We Call Bad Decisions "Poor Choices"

- If I decided to not finish high school, let alone college and graduate school, would I not have made a "poor choice" that would have greatly reduced my standard of living?

- If I decided to goof off on the job or not show up at all, would I not be making a "poor choice" resulting in me scrambling to find a new source of income?

- If I chose to ignore the law and decided instead to consume illegal drugs and/or large amounts of alcohol, would I not be making a "poor choice" that might cost innocent lives as well as my personal freedom?

- If I decided to have sex without proper birth control, would I not be making a "poor choice" that would require massive amounts of money to adequately support the children I produced?

Two More Questions:

- Is it ethical to pass the cost of these "poor choices" onto those who didn't make them?

- Isn't it responsible accountability by all that makes possible "liberty and justice for all?"

I believe that the most insidious form of child abuse is anything that denies a child their rightful progression to adulthood.

Parents who do their kids' homework while the youngsters go out to play are setting them up to fail. So, too, is a society that enables people to grow up to become perpetually irresponsible.

Public Assistance
Is About Assisting

Public assistance was never intended to assume ownership of other people's lives and their problems nor was it created to smother folks with disempowering pity. To the contrary, it was created to help people get on their feet. The problem is that we have tended to confuse lift chairs with recliners. Though they may look the same, their functions couldn't be further apart. One is designed to help one recline while the other is designed to help one stand. The first takes a person and tilts them back until they are completely at rest. The latter takes a person from a position of rest and lifts them up until they are on their feet. But it doesn't stop there. It keeps on going until it dumps the person forward, leaving them only two choices-to stand or fall flat.

The Example of
my Childhood

I was blessed with the world's greatest mother, ever! Sorry, global population, but don't feel bad; you really never had a chance as there never really was any competition. That being said, during my earliest years, she was away for protracted periods of time due to issues that were eventually resolved.

Anyway, with the very best of intentions, my brother and sister moved themselves into the spot of taking care of their youngest sibling even though we were each only 15 months apart in age. Like most toddlers and adolescents, I craved the love that came my way as a result of being their little work in progress and thrived on the attention they gave me. If I wanted sugar for my cereal or jelly for my toast, I'd barely look that way and they'd run and fetch it. It was great!

There was a downside, however. They hovered so closely that they were actually finishing my sentences before I had a chance to get my words out. In due course, I looked to them to accomplish anything and everything and never ventured out myself.

By the time they went off to school, I had become so dependent on them that I wouldn't dream of turning on the television set as they were the ones who always did it. The same was true about eating fruit. My brother and sister thought nothing of grabbing an orange or tangerine whenever they wanted it, peeling it and gobbling it down, but I had become so accustomed to going to them and having them feed me that I went without if they didn't provide for me.

Now notice, no one ever diagnosed me as being deficient in any way, but their overzealous love for me put me in such a weakened position, a position of perpetual dependence that now, fifty some years later, I still at times have to break through it just to stand on my own. And this is exactly what the well intentioned among us do with the "poor" and "disadvantaged."

We place them in a false reality where the copayment for medication is 50 cents, doctor's visits and hospitalizations are basically free and public housing is a far cry from the days of "the projects". Then, we sit back and wonder why initiative is lacking.

Just as I was saved by my brother and sister going to school, so, too, the "poor" among us would best be served by us going back to school on this one. We do them no favors by taking healthy, intelligent human beings and reducing them to virtual wards of the state. They will not only get on their feet, but reach for the stars if we would just stop providing incentives that keep them stuck in their dependency.

The problem with our way of helping is that it:

1) Assumes inability on the part of the recipient.

2) It limits growth as it threatens to withdraw at the first signs of independence.

3) Leaves the recipient weaker and more vulnerable than before we intervened, as the skills and strengths that were present at birth slowly atrophy (lose strength) due to a lack of usage. This eventually renders the person less able to function independently.

A Fatal Flaw in the War on Poverty

No matter how one slices and dices it, the fact remains that to achieve success in life, we need two ingredients: "opportunity" and "responsibility".

Opportunity was sorely lacking fifty years ago when the Rev. Dr. Martin Luther King, Jr. led the March on Washington. Thankfully, it is a very different story today. All kinds of barriers have been broken down and doors have been opened. We as a society, as a nation, are better for it.

Responsibility can be defined as owning the opportunities that life gives us and working with them to improve our situation. Where the "War on Poverty" got off track was when it took opportunity and made it into something entirely different, namely "entitlement." People have been led to feel "entitled" to guaranteed incomes, increasingly nicer and nicer housing, free health care and the like, whether or not they take advantage of the opportunities given them or not.

The Constitution guarantees citizens equal access to opportunities. It does not and cannot guarantee these opportunities will yield the same results for all because we each bring our own set of gifts, talents and baggage to whatever we attempt in life.

We've Set Out on the Ultimate Fool's Errand

While the rest of society knows that the key to success is an investment of time and energy coupled with a certain amount of risk, the poor have been given the message that they somehow live in a different reality where the blessings continue regardless of whether they are industrious or not.

It shouldn't take a Nobel Prize in Economics to recognize the underlying premise of any economy is that everyone is operating with the same system of rewards and the same carrots in front of everyone's horses. To do otherwise and set up an alternative framework where whole segments of a population are working with a different set of financial assumptions is to embark on a fool's errand. It is every bit as ridiculous as having runners in the same race set off in divergent directions for different finish lines.

Yet, that is exactly what we have in this country today. For while the majority of us have been raised with the understanding that the harder one works the better quality of life one is able to enjoy and the nicer the neighborhood one is able to live in, millions of others are proving every day that the exact opposite is true for them. We all know of untold numbers of situations where people basically goof off, "hang out" and sabotage opportunity after opportunity and still can count on getting a monthly check in the mail.

As a result, some, certainly not all, but quite a few are content to stay where they are or fall even further behind lest they lose the "benefits" to which they have been repeatedly told they are entitled.

The folly in this is that by always cushioning their fall, we have taken away the initiative that is essential to growth. We are no different than the parent that fights all of their kid's battles and takes on all of their challenges. It may satisfy the parents' need to feel helpful, but make no mistake about it, this dynamic denies the child a crucial component of their development.

At some point, no matter how benevolent and generous people choose to be, this enabling will have to stop once those who rise to an alarm clock and go to work reach the end of their collective credit limit and society as a whole is no longer able to borrow the money to keep the handouts going. What will happen then? What on earth will become of the poor?

The following are photographs of government subsidized housing in my neck of the woods.

Some units are detached, some are duplexes and others are condominium-like in appearance. All are immaculately landscaped and maintained by ground crews.

Assignment:

Drive around your neighborhood. Find housing complexes with the HUD symbol on the sign. The HUD symbol is identical in shape to the plastic Monopoly game piece that one places on the board to charge rent to those who land on owned property. The only difference is that the outline of the HUD house has an = sign drawn inside of it.

You'll be shocked to see that many are strikingly attractive mission style homes or apartment complexes with "cultured stone" facades, "architectural style" shingle roofs and new or newer cars parked out front. They have been placed in middle or even upper class neighborhoods as a way to doing away with the "stigma" of public housing.

We Need To Stop Thinking
These People Are Helpless

We are now approaching fifty years since President Lyndon Johnson declared a war on poverty. The impoverished children of the 1960's are now grandparents or, in some cases, great grandparents themselves. I doubt very much that MLK and LBJ ever intended to create a permanent welfare class. Instead, they merely wanted to give folks the opportunity to attain the full potential that already existed within them.

Example of a Rowing Coach Empowering the Team

When a rowing team is doing poorly, the coach doesn't climb into the boat, grab the oar and instruct the rowers to sit back and go for a ride while he starts pulling on the oar. No! He or she starts yelling words of encouragement from the shoreline and starts putting into play exercises that will help the team get the proper conditioning that is necessary to start pulling ahead. Our problem is that with the best of intentions, we do just the opposite. We tell people they can't do it alone, and in so doing, we unwittingly make them all the more dependent.

Why Independence and Freedom Are Interchangeable

Listen to the language. See how often our founding fathers and later voices such as the late Rev. Dr. Martin Luther King, Jr. have used the above mentioned words interchangeably when speaking of political freedom and human liberation. The reason is simple. People cannot truly be free until they establish their independence and self-sufficiency. As long as they have to depend on others, they are not autonomous, but controlled by them and subject to their bidding.

We should have people in publicly subsidized housing continue to pay the same amounts they have always paid, but starting immediately, these folks will go from renters to homeowners. This way, people who would never qualify for a home loan otherwise, will start to build up equity that will translate into a nest egg for when they retire.

The only stipulation is that the government will immediately get out of the housing business. No longer will our society attack problems in reverse. Gone will be the days of us looking at the number of children in a family and then deciding how many bedrooms to provide for them. It doesn't work that way for wage earners; why should it work that way for non-wage earners? No, from here on out, a person will have to either limit the number of children they bring into the world or increase their income to be able to care for them. Currently, the people least able to feed their children are the ones most likely to bear them. That is backwards and only perpetuates cruel, multi-generational poverty that blesses no one, least of all the children born of it.

Lest people profit from our charitable acts: Occupants will only be able to sell and keep the proceeds from these homes when one of two things happen: (1) the total cost of the unit has been paid in full, or (2) the person reaches retirement age and takes out the equity they have built up as they move into a retirement setting. Prior to paying off the cost of the home, all proceeds from the sale of these units will be automatically reapplied to the purchase of another home until the same conditions are met.

These are good, solid, first steps toward true autonomy. They are essential, for if there is one thing history tells us, it is that the feelings of the crowd are fickle. The same people that shout hosanna one day may well be in an entirely different mood, but a few days later. Be grateful for what is given you, but don't rely on it. It's best to make your own way and be dependent on no one.

We Should Take a Good Hard Look at Our Financial Aid System

1) *Under existing programs, we have people who are skilled at having us care for them.* If we reduce the amount of assistance we offer,

they just lower their standard of living. If we create massive labyrinths of regulations complete with checks and balances to make sure the money is going to its intended purpose, they become adept at "working the system" instead of ever actually working.

2) ***All of this goes on while other people suffer a major crisis and don't qualify for help.*** They need immediate intervention, but they don't meet the criteria for public assistance as the equity in their home classifies them as having too many assets to receive our help. These individuals have to first lose everything including their house that they have spent an entire lifetime acquiring before our charitable arm swings into action.

This is as ludicrous as it is unfair. It all boils down to this. Folks whose only visible means of support is the government might not own their place of residence, but they have even more security than those of us who do. For while the average wage earner is but a paycheck away from default on their home loans, those who are idle and have been for years are guaranteed perpetual shelter. Not only that, they are also shielded from the headache of figuring out how to pay for costly repairs such as replacing a roof, furnace or major appliance.

Apparently it isn't enough for someone to just need help with a few medical bills. No, we aren't set up to deal with that. Instead, we wait and let them go without any kind help until they are too sick to work and lose everything. Then, instead of just meeting a simple medical need, we are saddled with a whole array of massive, complex medical needs plus the responsibility of providing both an income and housing.

This isn't only financially devastating to those who could have regained their footing with just a little help. It is also financially devastating to our entire economy as many of these recipients are then given the message to stay below certain income levels in order to continue receiving help. This makes them all the more dependent for virtually forever and leaves fewer workers in the tax base to carry the burden of more and more families. In short, our approach really and truly meets the classic definition of being penny wise and pound foolish.

Right now, there's no connection between welfare and personal responsibility

I know of a situation where one of the members of a close friend's family had a severe but manageable medical condition. The intensity of the symptoms could have been minimized to the point of being almost negligible had the individual chosen to comply with easy to follow medical advice. Unfortunately, almost from day one, this person did just about everything but follow doctor's orders. As a result, an award could have probably been won for the most repeat hospital admissions in the nation (had there been such an award), the overwhelming majority of which were entirely preventable. Indeed, this person's life provides an excellent case study of what happens when we bear ultimate responsibility for people who refuse to take any responsibility for their own lives.

In addition to the countless medical bills racked up since the onset of the disease, there was a couple of year stretch where the individual would barely return home from intensive care before repeating the same practices that put the person in the hospital in the first place. This resulted in calling yet another ambulance to transport the same individual back to the same hospital, often the same intensive care unit, where the whole cycle would start all over again. For a few years, this was repeated on an almost weekly basis.

There's little doubt in my mind that taxpayers easily spent a couple of million dollars in hospital bills alone just because of this one person's conscious decision to be medically non-compliant. In addition, this same person collected public assistance as the head of a household with children and lived in a home built by a charity.

The height of it for me, however, was when it was disclosed during a family meeting that on one occasion nobody was responding to her repeated requests for a drink of water. Undeterred, she called 911. An ambulance was dispatched and soon a nice cold bottle of water was provided by emergency responders (at taxpayers' expense).

How Can This Happen?

The answer is simple. There is nothing to stop it. Our society has been so overwhelmed by guilt for its horrific sins of the past that it has become hyperextended in its attempt to make amends. The result has been the creation of a false reality where the expense of housing, healthcare and higher education are heavily (and I mean heavily) subsidized. Even if copays for medical needs are never paid (and often times they are not) the care continues because we have engineered all of the consequences out of the equation.

As for the rest of us wage earners, regardless of how much we pay, or even offer to pay an insurance company, none of us could come remotely close to recreating this same "hospital rotation" because no policy is offered without of a system of copayments and deductibles that are just high enough to make us think twice before setting up an appointment or calling an ambulance. In short, they have made us wise medical consumers. This has saved them, us and the whole industry untold billions of dollars.

While the poor are insulated from further decline regardless of their actions, workers have to pay for everyone else's "What Ifs." Just look at their paystubs!

There's the:

- "What if I become injured on the job?" contingency covered by Worker's Comp.

- "What if I or a member of my family get sick?" contingency covered by health insurance.

- And finally the, "What if total strangers, people in the general population get sick or injured?" contingency covered by federal, state and county tax withholdings.

What Does All of This Mean?

It means the people who bear the burden for most of these benefits, the middle class, are the very ones least likely to receive them.

A Flat Income Tax, Not Sales Tax, Is the Most Fair

On the surface, a flat sales tax sounds the most equitable and fair, but it actually favors the rich because at some juncture, wealthy people purchase all they need and want. From then on, the vast majority of their earnings go into enormous stockpiles of capital, while others live paycheck to paycheck and spend just about every dollar they bring home.

It reminds me of the dilemma many of us face when shopping for a gift to give our fathers on birthdays and holidays. Idea after idea is tossed aside as we realize he already has it, and if he doesn't, it's only because he probably doesn't want it. So, we come up short, stumped by that age old question, "What do you give the man who already has everything?"

Believe it or not, there are a lot of people, not just men, who fall into this category. They have more than enough, and yet, are still pulling ahead of the rest of us in their earning power. If we only collected sales taxes, the people at the top would pay a far smaller percentage of their incomes than those who barely eek-out an existence.

While it hardly seems fair to penalize the rich for succeeding, it also isn't fair that the rich pay little or nothing. A "flat income tax" instead of a "flat sales tax" is the solution. For then, everyone would pay the same percentage of their incomes regardless of whether or not they spend the income they accrue.

Let's Back Up and Start From Scratch

Imagine a society where, because we no longer offshore our industrial production, American workers have the opportunity to earn more than enough to support their families (as they once did) on a single paycheck. On these incomes and the incomes earned by private enterprises as well as massive corporations, the same fixed, across the board tax is collected.

A Tax System like This, Based on Tithing, Is Fairest

It certainly seems to work for God (and I am not being flippant here, but to the contrary, very sincere.) The way tithing works in the Judeo-Christian understanding is that a flat 10% of all income is required. This is across the board, regardless of standing. It is due off the top, before anyone gets their hands on it. The beauty of this is in its proportionality. 10% of a million bucks is just as hard for a millionaire to swallow as the 10% assessed the white collar worker and the 10% assessed the pauper. Think about it.

This Will Greatly Reduce the Cost of the IRS

This tax plan also saves a whole heap of money, and I mean a really, really big, whole heap of a lot of bunches of money by immediately simplifying our tax code. No longer will we be supporting an ever burgeoning Internal Revenue Service with its legions of accountants and tax attorneys tasked with determining which "loopholes" are legal and which are not. This step alone will save the government bazillions and bazillions of dollars in administrative costs once everyone, and I mean everyone, pays the same percentage into the system, be they rich or poor, wholesale or retail, wage earner or investor, mega corporation, or mom and pop business. If the changes that I suggest in the next few pages are implemented, then it may be possible to get down to a low, tolerable rate. Whatever it is, the percentage should be the same for each contributor.

This engages the poor and gives them a sense of ownership. As it is now, a sizeable percentage of our population couldn't care less if tax revenues are squandered. It isn't their money. Once they begin paying into it, however, then they will have the same guttural reaction that I, as a taxpayer, had when I heard an ambulance had actually been summoned because no one was heeding a plea for a glass of water. Anytime we can broaden the citizens' sense of ownership in this or any democracy, it is a good thing in and of itself.

As good, honest people, I believe the following:

- We want to encourage motivation, not complacency.

- While we don't want people to go without, we also don't want to reward irresponsible, reckless behavior.

- We want to get aid to people quickly, then have they step up to the plate and cancel it once their immediate need is met and they no longer need outside help to survive.

The Need to Start Fresh

Sometimes in life, it is much more expeditious and cost effective to back out of current approaches altogether and start fresh than it is to keep trying to make things work. It's like an airplane attempting to land. Sometimes it will come in too high or too low, too fast or at the wrong angle or pitch, and the control tower will radio the pilot with instructions to circle around and make another attempt. Or, more germane to our individual experience, it's like trying to parallel park a car. If one starts from a weird angle or distance from the curb, it is much easier to pull out of the spot altogether and start fresh all over again.

OK, Then, How Do We Help Without Creating Dependency?

In the final analysis, the best way to assist people without stifling their God given instinct to struggle to survive is to transition them away from passively receiving that for which they have not worked. This will encourage people to make wiser choices and take personal responsibility for the paths they choose. When this happens, I believe we'll begin to see more people attain their potential as autonomous, self-directed human beings.

We Need A Happy Medium Between Life Before Roosevelt When People Could Die in the Gutter and Today When People Become Lifelong Wards of the State.

A Fresh Approach

We need to figure out a way to pry off the ceilings that for decades have stymied personal achievement and held our economy back. Think of all the people we personally know who would love to pick up a few more dollars, but don't dare because it will mean the loss of unemployment benefits, a public assistance check or place people in a tax bracket where their income goes from being a blessing to being a burden.

The sum total of all of these millions of situations easily comes to billions and billions of dollars. It's an astronomical sum. We're not only talking about the loss of all of that taxable revenue, but also the cost of continuing to support millions and millions of people who, failing to rise to the occasion, have limited themselves and, therefore, continued to depend on us to feed, clothe and house them. The cost to our GNP (Gross National Product) has been incalculable.

The Solution is Twofold

First: Eliminate Ceilings and Caps
Second: Create Contingency/Rainy Day Accounts

Some will immediately respond that without ceilings and caps there will be no reason for people to stop collecting unemployment and other benefits. To which I respond, they will stop once they realize they are only spending down or depleting money that has been steadily growing with in their own Contingency/Rainy Day Savings Accounts. This is how I see these accounts working.

Instead of having our tax dollars go into a vast pool that we can't access…why not set up a Rainy Day Savings plan that people can make withdrawals from as needed? Each taxable unit (person or company) will contribute an equal percentage from their sources of revenue. They will be automatically deducted from each paycheck with a running total showing on each paystub. From this savings pool, funds can be used for those unexpected things all of us run into.

If we get laid off from work, the funds are there to carry us for a while. If we need to finance college tuition, we have funds we can draw on. If our parent needs to go into a nursing home, then, we have access to money already set aside. If wiped out by a bankruptcy or house fire or stroke, there is money to help us get back on our feet. If these accounts are ever exhausted, the system borrows money from other accounts where those funds are not yet needed.

These personal "Rainy Day Accounts" are not automatically made accessible. Only certain specific and out of the ordinary needs qualify for making these monies available.

What About When
The Rainy Day Accounts Dry Up?

The system will continue to pay out until certain thresholds are met. At these junctures, one of three things will happen. The individual will submit a reasonable action plan for repayment. If none is forthcoming, the person will be assigned a task to support the public good with the proceeds going directly to paying off the loan to the system.

If the individual is unable to come up with a feasible action plan and is physically unable to work due to justifiable medical limitations, then a forbearance can be granted to postpone or forgive the debt altogether.

Consider for a moment what happens to the mindset of people when they go from welfare recipients who have to play the role of being poor enough to continue in the program to being just like everyone else in society.

Instead of figuring out how to get more and more out of the system by being societal beggars, they now have a motivation to take control and make wise decisions. Again, just imagine what people can and will do once they see their savings grow and realize they can also add to it beyond their payroll deductions. This will foster motivation instead of the defeatist message currently given that (1) they are poor and (2) they will be penalized if they so much as make any financial progress.

The goal is to put responsibility where it belongs, not on strangers, not on the society at large, but on individuals who in this day and age have more than ample opportunities to care for themselves and their families...if they do not squander them.

If for no other reason than the well-being of the recipients, the days of codependent coddling must end and end now, before those who are currently paying all of the bills reach the end of their ropes and stop it altogether. It is far more humane to transition people to self-sufficiency while there is still ample means of support in place to aid the transition.

More Benefits
of This Program

People will no longer have reason to judge the way others, particularly the poor, spend money, as ultimately, it comes out of their own pocket thanks to the sweat of their brow.

If they want to live in a run down, dilapidated residence with an enormous, top-of-the line, wide screen television in the living room, and a late model car in the driveway, so be it. It's their money and, accordingly, no one else's business to pass judgment, as long as, of course, the needs of the children and other dependents in that home are met.

Even if there are a good number of people who are truly incapacitated and qualify for forbearance on the monies they will be given plus the promise of a continual infusion of financial aid, it will be far less than the number we are currently carrying who have no expectation of either ending their dependency or repaying monies they are receiving. Yet, this is just the beginning of the true societal benefits.

Consider for a moment all of the illegal activities that "the poor" currently justify engaging in as they know that verifiable incomes such as a "real job", will mean the end of getting public assistance. In light of this, there is a whole underground economy going on as these individuals, like the rest of us, have the desire to have money in their pockets.

If we take away the incentive to hide incomes and remain poor enough (at least on paper) to get help, then we have hope of motivating people to earn and save even more. As it is now, a lot of people are telling themselves they have to engage in activities they know deep down inside are wrong as they have no other choice.

What Happens To Unused Funds?

I would propose the establishment of a timetable of five year blocks. If a person is able to maintain a percentage of savings in that account, let's say 80%, then they can withdraw 20% of it for a durable good or product. A durable good or product is here defined as something that will enhance their life in the long run. Do the math, this can add up to a sizeable amount of money. It can be applied toward the purchase of a car, the down payment on a house, the investment in a Roth IRA or a business – anything that is not an indulgence. Funds not used at the end of a life, when money is most likely needed for nursing home care etc., will be returned to the general fund.

Do you see where this is going? It singlehandedly promotes responsible behavior and financial planning, while at the same time, taking away any incentive for being a couch potato. From now on, inaction will no longer result in an automatic handout. The availability of capital grows in each worker's "Rainy Day Fund" and America is off and running once again. In short, it puts the poorest among us right where they should be, in the real world, not some fictitious reality based on the generosity of strangers that can be easily withdrawn.

In this is the affirmation of their abilities, the very thing the present system lacks. For the current underlying assumption is that the poor are never going to be able to make it on their own. It assumes they will never break the surface and be able to keep their financial heads above water. This is why we equip them with gills like a fish so that at least they won't drown under water. Once so equipped, we have doomed them to intergenerational dependence, for now their struggle is not to get back on solid ground, but rather to stay in the well-stocked pond we have artificially made for them lest they suffocate like "a fish out of water" in the real world the rest of us encounter every day.

Don't believe it? Presently the system is set up so that if a "poor person" increases their income too much, they will lose their publicly supported housing, their incredible publicly supported health care benefits and of course their monthly check and food stamps.

If we really want to reduce the number of people in poverty, we also need to:

1) Close the wage gaps. There is no way those at the top can justify making hundreds of times the salary of the the average worker, yet it goes on all of the time and must be stopped. Honest work deserves good honest pay, period.

2) Give people a chance at a fresh start. Currently, a lot of people are unemployed because they drag a police record around with them for the rest of their lives. Whatever happened to paying one's debt to society and then having a clean slate?

3) Enforce usury laws. Put a lid on outrageous interest rates charged by loan sharks and credit card companies. These keep people in financial servitude. Rein them in immediately.

4) Make it illegal to drop out of school. Just as the law now requires attendance up until the ninth grade, make it mandatory to complete high school (even if the student gets pregnant).

5) This practice of women raising children with Uncle Sam as the bread winner does little more than promote irresponsible behavior. Children

need men in their lives. Restore the role of fathers as responsible providers.

The Biggest Barriers to Affordable Healthcare:

 # 1) Insurance   **# 3) Endless Documentation**

 # 2) Attorneys   **# 4) Inflated Charges**

Just as the greatest expense in building a home is not the cost of the land, nor the materials, nor even the labor, but rather, the cost of financing the mortgage, so, too, the greatest expenses in medicine is not paying for the doctors and nurses, nor medicine and infrastructure, but rather, the costs that have literally nothing to do with actually healing the body.

What was the most expensive war?
The Cold War…
~A war that was never fought~

What is medicine's greatest expense?
Health and Liability/malpractice insurance…
Paying for what may never happen.

Background:

I remember riding down the road in the back seat of my mom's Rambler in the early 1970s listening to a discussion on the radio over whether or not to allow lawyers to advertise their services. At the time, I remember thinking to myself, "What harm could it possibly do?" Boy was I mistaken! That decision to allow the legal profession the right to grow their businesses through ad campaigns has deeply impacted all of our lives. It has added a surcharge, not at all unlike a tax, onto every human activity under the sun and transformed this nation from a right friendly place in which to live into a land of ambulance chasers complete with distrust among neighbors. It is sheer madness.

I use the word "madness" deliberately as MAD, or "Mutually Assured Destruction," was the theory that prevailed during the Cold War. In a nutshell, it basically said that as long as both sides produced weapons at roughly the same rate of speed, the world would remain safe as no one in their right mind would ever "push the button," because it would result in our "mutually assured destruction."

For years and years, this approach worked (kind of). True, no one ever did push the button, but it was the unsustainable cost of the arms race itself that ultimately did destroy one of the players.

The Soviets couldn't keep up with continually buying more and more "insurance" and so, finally, their whole system collapsed. The parallels between their plight and the escalating cost of our litigious society cannot be ignored. In both cases, enormous amounts of money are spent, but not a dime of it leads to increased goods and services. It's like paying rent. Once the money is gone, it's gone, and there is nothing to show for it.

Theoretical Benefit of Ambulance Chasers

"Lawyers keep the medical profession on its toes. They are the watchdogs protecting us from sloppy healthcare. Without them, quality would plummet" or at least, so they'd have us think. In reality, lawyers have diverted a lot of time, energy and money away from medical care to protecting doctors from the very same threat of litigation lawyers have themselves created.

Today, a doctor's biggest financial expense is medical malpractice insurance, and a practice's biggest expenditure of time is on charting designed not so much to heal the patient as much as it is to prevent lawsuits. Additionally, the biggest motivation for excessive tests, scans and lab work is the fear of litigation. This all adds up to what we now call "defensive medicine."

Lawyers' unquenchable thirst for more and more business has taken their "get rich through litigation" campaigns beyond doctors, hospitals, and nursing homes to pharmaceutical companies and medical device manufacturers as well. As a result, the across the board cost for every aspect of health care has skyrocketed. Even if we don't run up expensive medical bills ourselves, Uncle Sam does by virtue of being the biggest healthcare consumer. Each month, the treasury sends out literally billions to cover these costs.

The theory behind "ambulance chasers" is that medical practitioners will, out of fear of massive judgments, provide the very best care possible. It sounds reasonable until one realizes the primary response to fear is not so much providing better care to others as much as it is providing better protection for one's self. Accordingly, resources have been reallocated away from patient care to the funding of higher medical liability coverage, increased documentation, and the prescribing of more and more lab work.

Under The Current System

Only the most obvious cases of medical neglect and malpractice with the potential for big money settlements glean the attention of attorneys. All of the other cases worthy of review are never granted a hearing. This is like having a hospital that only treats lucrative cancer and heart attack cases, but passes up on everything else.

Non-medical people (lawyers) try medical cases before other non- medical people (jurors). This makes perfect sense if the intention is to appeal to the emotions in order to win bigger verdicts, but it makes little sense if the objective is to actually improve medical care. Court verdicts might impact wallets, but seldom impact a physician's ability to practice medicine. Even if a license is suspended, a doctor can move to another state and start over.

A local attorney is currently advertising that he has collected over $420 million dollars in damages. That's nearly half a billion dollars! Now, remember that is just one law office here in SW Georgia.

Multiply that by all of the law firms nationwide in the same line of work and watch the amounts skyrocket.

Finally, factor in all of the money bilked out of the system by drug manufacturers and medical supply companies. Drugs manufactured here cost American consumers infinitely more than anywhere else in the world. Why? It is because they can get away with it. Uncle Sam will pay just about any bill that is submitted…even when it is blatantly clear that the figures are grossly inflated.

As one who has spent many years in the medical field, first, promoting organ and tissue donation and as a hospice chaplain, I can tell you that fear of litigation is the last thing that we want in medicine. In its presence, opportunities for real improvement are squandered and already limited resources are diverted from patient care to excessive documentation. Hours upon hours upon hours are diverted from caring for patients and re-allocated to diminishing the threat of potential litigation.

I firmly believe that the solution to better health care starts with an agreement. I'd just bet that if only lawyers promised to stay out of medical settings, doctors and nurses would only be more than happy to stay out of their courtrooms. It's just that simple!

Other Ways to Improve Healthcare

Currently, we limit the number of hours a pilot can be in a cockpit or a tractor trailer driver can be behind the wheel, but there are no regulations for how long a person can be on shift as a physician.

Part of the standard medical training is to be a "resident" at a hospital. What a descriptive term! It says it all. These students are required to work virtually round the clock and basically reside at the hospital with virtually little or no sleep. We then expect them to make sound, rational life and death decisions for caseloads of patients that would confound even the most seasoned of physicians.

Is that smart? These students are just becoming acquainted with the conditions they are now thrust into dealing with and expected to write prescriptions when many of them are too tired to even drive a car. I could see it if they were being trained to serve in a combat setting where replacements might be 36 hours away, but this isn't the case. Instead, it is hospitals cashing in on the savings they get by virtue of stretching physicians past the normal limits of human endurance. It's bad medicine, plain and simple.

In a similar vein, we all know of doctors who take on more patients then they can handle. For example, I am acquainted with a number of physicians who have assumed roles as medical directors of this, that and the other plus run their own sprawling medical practices plus, plus, plus. The way they do it is simple, they have their nurse practitioners and physician assistants do a lot of the work under their moniker. The fee they charge is just the same, but the consumer gets a less qualified practitioner seeing them.

In every endeavor there eventually comes into play a law of diminishing returns and I think healthcare is too important to not address this issue. Public safety demands it.

Nursing Homes

These facilities collect astronomical amounts of money whether the care is compassionate and delivered in a timely manner or not. Families who depend on them are often placed in the awful position of watching their loved ones suffer because some, certainly not all, but some of the staff members are not oriented toward compassion and mercy. Rather, they are frighteningly able to tune out patients who are calling out for their help. They act as though they don't see the obvious and can't hear reasonable requests for help.

Why does this go on? Why do patients and family members feel so powerless? It's because payment doesn't come directly from them. Rather it comes through their insurance, Medicare or Medicaid. Once these bureaucracies get a bill, the facility is paid even if the care is lousy by any standard.

I have been in nursing homes for most of my vocational career and I believe the answer is simple. It is having the facility become directly accountable to the people they serve. How does this happen? Empower recipients and their families to do what customers do in every other situation, namely pay only for the services rendered. Let me explain...

I think nursing homes should automatically get 90% of what they charge. That's a given. The remaining ten percent will be sent if and only if for that calendar month, the facility gets a 60% or better favorability rating by the people they serve. (That's more than fair as 60% would translate into a D in academic circles.)

The rating will be determined by an anonymous survey conducted by an independent organization with no vested interest on either side of the fence. The payment will be for the remaining 10% or nothing. Slicing it down into smaller percentages will only detract from the facility's urgent desire to do whatever is necessary to improve patient care and to do it quickly.

We now have patients with spotless charts and soiled sheets. Why? It is because health care is so busy operating on the negative energy of fear of lawsuits that it has neither the time nor the resources to focus on healing.

Universal Health Care? Dealing With the "Yeah, Buts..."

Like it or not, universal healthcare is already here (and has been here for some time) as evidenced by the fact that it is illegal for hospitals to deny medical care to anyone. The dollars are already being spend.

The question is, do we want our money to continue to go to insurers, lawyers and pharmaceutical giants or do we want to heal the sick, all of the sick and nothing but the sick… and do it all for much, much, much less money than the sum total we as a society currently spend on supposed "health care?" We can easily afford to pay for present realities, it is the fear of the "what if's" that is bankrupting us.

The Biggest Fear that Holds Us Back From Reaping the Benefits:

Yeah, but once you bring in everyone, you include people who have very little to contribute and who are most likely have an extensive backlog of medical problems that, in short order, will bankrupt the whole system.

Rebuttal: On the surface, it would seem so, but as mentioned earlier, all insurance carriers have built in mechanisms specifically designed to prevent this exact same thing from happening. They are called deductibles and co-pays. This requirement of making patients pay a portion of the cost for services rendered could be included in universal healthcare so that it is protected from frivolous over-usage.

Think about it. There are a lot of things I'd love to have medically checked out, but don't dare because I don't want to pay the deductible. Accordingly, I now think long and hard before running to the doctor, ER or even calling an ambulance. It is because even though I am fully insured, the costs not covered by my medical insurance (deductibles and co-pays) are high enough to make me a wise and frugal medical consumer. We can build the same co-pays into any universal plan we create, thereby protecting it from the same threat of needless over usage.

Again, whether we like it or not, we as a society are already paying for universal health care. The question is, what is the quality of that care and could we get more bang out of our buck if such a high percentage of it wasn't first siphoned off by non-medical opportunists.

In conclusion,
Why We're Out of Kilter,
Fixing America's Feng Shui

Feng Shui, the Chinese study of energy fields, speaks directly, I believe, to what is going on in our country today. It suggests that we have unwittingly set up opposing lines of energy that hinder virtually all we currently attempt in this our *United* States of America.

I mean, really, just look at us. Our political parties have divided us right down the middle and polarized us so much that most Americans think, act and vote as if our enemies are not external, but rather the other half of our fellow citizens. A perfect example of this is Bush I writing off half of the electorate by routinely referring to them as "the L word"…a group of people too profane to even mention. Talk about oppositional energy!

Then look at our societal response to poverty. We trap people in "the system" by seducing them with the message that what they need to do isn't pull ahead, but rather remain poor enough to keep on receiving assistance. *Remaining helpless enough to get help?* Look at that for just a moment. The very logic contained therein couldn't be more oppositional if it tried.

Finally, there's our motivation for health care. We have developed an entire medical system based on the ultimate application of grotesque oppositional energy. It goes like this. We will receive good care, not because anyone cares about us; no, love and compassion have nothing to do with it. We will receive good care because if we don't get it, we'll turn around and sue the pants off of those who should have provided it. What better example could there be of trying to get what we want, not by positive initiation, but rather the heartless application of oppositional energy.

None of this is working! I plead with each and every one of you, don't succumb to the lie that we as common, everyday citizens are powerless to turn this thing around. Those who have painted us into this corner want us to believe it. They want us to believe that we have no option, but to return them to power as only they have the necessary experience to govern.

Baloney feathers! We have had plenty of experience. We've experienced them taking a perfectly strong, healthy and robust country and drive it into the ground. The founding fathers had no experience with running a democracy, it was all new to them. But they had one thing that the powers that once ruled them never came close to having, a vision of and a hunger for a government of the people, by the people and for the people.

A Simple 10 Point Plan
to Rescue America

1) *Elect a decisive President who is truly independent and not tied in to either party.*

2) *Have him/her work to reduce the influence of political parties.*

3) *Get rid of all lobbyist loot. Have the government allocate 100% of all election funds with a reasonable budget given each campaign.*

4) *Illegalize deal making in passing legislation. Make it just as illegal to buy or trade votes in Congress as it is on Election Day.*

5) *Make every citizen's vote truly count. Dump the Electoral College.*

6) *Stop being chicken! Stand up to China before it is too late!*

7) *Make America our most favored nation. Reopen our factories now.*

8) *Be the very best of neighbors to Mexico. Send them ridiculous amounts of foreign aid, but don't legitimize illegal immigrants.*

9) *Establish the same rights and obligations to all citizens.*

10) *Get past the guilt trips. Enjoy life, liberty and the pursuit of happiness.*

LIST OF HEADINGS

www.ingramcontent.com/pod-product-compliance
Lightning Source LLC
Chambersburg PA
CBHW070802290526
45795CB00002B/597